Two days after the worldwide demonstrations against the Iraq war on February 15 2003, New York Times *reporter Patrick Tyler wrote that* "The huge anti-war demonstrations around the world this weekend are reminders that there may still be two superpowers on the planet: The United States and world public opinion."

In the UK the Stop the War Coalition remains the focal point of that public opinion, as does United for Peace and Justice in America. As the Pentagon publishes its plans for a Long War on many continents and the spin doctors continue to ratchet up tension and fear, the mobilization of the peoples of the world against war is as urgent and necessary as ever.

This book is part of that movement.

NOT ONE MORE DEATH

VERSO

NOT ONE MORE DEATH

Brian Eno

John le Carré

Harold Pinter

Richard Dawkins

Haifa Zangana

Michel Faber

VERSO

London • New York

First published by Verso 2006
Not One More Death © Verso and
Stop the War Coalition 2006

Not One More Death conceived and compiled by Anthea Eno and
David Wilson for the Stop the War Coalition

3 5 7 9 10 8 6 4 2

Verso
UK: 6 Meard Street, London W1F 0EG
USA: 180 Varick Street, New York, NY 10014–4606
www.versobooks.com

Verso is the imprint of New Left Books

ISBN-10: 1-84467-116-X

ISBN-13: 978-1-84467-116-8

British Library Cataloguing in Publication Data
A catalogue record for this book is available from
the British Library

Library of Congress Cataloging-in-Publication Data
A catalog record for this book is available from
the Library of Congress

Cover Design by David Wardle
Typeset in Sabon by New Left Review

Printed in the UK by Cox and Wyman Ltd, Reading, Berkshire

Contents

Notes on the Authors

John le Carré's most recent book is *Absolute Friends*. His nineteen novels include *The Constant Gardener*.

Richard Dawkins is the Charles Simonyi Professor of the Public Understanding of Science at Oxford University. He is the author of *The Selfish Gene* and, most recently, *The Ancestor's Tale*.

Brian Eno's albums include *Another Green World* and *Apollo: Atmospheres and Soundtracks*; he has also produced artists such as U2 and David Bowie.

Michel Faber is the author of *The Crimson Petal and the White* and *The Fahrenheit Twins*.

Harold Pinter was awarded the 2005 Nobel Prize for Literature.

Haifa Zangana is an Iraqi-born novelist, artist and activist; her books include *Keys to a City* and *Women on a Journey*.

BRIAN ENO

The Missionary Position

THE DEFINING event of the last ten years was the fraudulent election of George Bush as President of the United States in 2000. It was the fruition of an anti-liberal reaction that had been working its way through the American social fabric for the previous thirty years. This reaction was dedicated to, and has to some extent succeeded in, unravelling Western democratic liberalism. We are now in the anti-sixties.

With America terrified after 9/11, and the media in a frenzy of paranoia, it was a foregone conclusion that a "tough," "no-nonsense" leader like Bush would look right to the American people. The cabal that Bush fronted – together with Cheney, Rumsfeld, Wolfowitz and Perle – had been manoeuvring itself into position throughout the nineties, and its members had made their intentions clear in the texts of "The Project for a New American Century" (PNAC) and elsewhere. They now looked forward to carte blanche, secure in the knowledge that anyone questioning their full-frontal assault on liberal democracy could be labelled as either naïve or treacherous and duly marginalized.

They believed in "full spectrum dominance," they believed in pre-emptive military action, but most of all they believed in the historical destiny of the United States and its right to assert and secure its hegemony. At root they thought that America had triumphed in the world not because it was powerful but because it was fundamentally *right,* and history had so judged. From there it was a short step to thinking that America had a divine duty to help the rest of the world emulate it, and to exclude or even punish those who wouldn't. This is the Missionary position.

Whatever had been achieved or aimed for in the sixties was what this new revolution now had in its sights, and was set to dismantle. "Market Forces" and "The Invisible Hand" – mysteriously guiding the self-organizing economic paradise – became deified, just as "Mother Nature" had been deified by the hippies thirty years earlier. This aggressive Market Romanticism brought with it a sort of missionary zeal indistinguishable from the drive to Christianize the world that occupied the nineteenth century and must at that time have seemed just as unarguably, self-evidently right. After all, as we would have said then, and as we are still saying now, it's for their own good.

Such were the preconditions for a war: the need for a sharply drawn world picture that includes a clear and evil enemy (the Soviet Union having stepped out of the picture); the assumption of absolute moral superiority; the unstoppable hunger of aggressive capitalism; a simplistic cause-and-effect idealism; and a lot of firepower. That moves the project on from Missionary to Crusader.

But it leaves two unanswered questions: what did Tony Blair have to do with all this, and how did he and Bush end up in Iraq of all places? Wasn't it al-Qaeda we were supposed to be after?

At the time, the kind explanation regarding the Blair/Bush betrothal was that Blair would rein in the worst impulses of the Bushmen – although this explanation faded as they ignored him whenever it suited them, and anyway it became clearer that he shared many of their millenarian impulses. Another theory held that Blair, an evangelical Christian like Bush, discovered a "kinship" with him in that they both understood what Good and Evil meant and were prepared to act without the dithering qualms and nuances that liberals or judges or teachers or civil servants or military officers (or indeed anyone with actual experience of life outside politics) might be inclined to show.

Perhaps the explanation is simpler. Blair is a man who admires charisma and power, and who wants to be around those who have them. He is, in short, a fan. He was bedazzled by the glamour of the Bush court, and by his own sudden debut on the world stage next to the President. It was his chance to be sidekick to the most powerful man on the planet, and for the two of them to preside triumphantly over the birth of a brave new world order, starting with Iraq. It was a vanity project. As time passes and the insiders begin to talk, it seems increasingly likely that simple male ego might have been the reason these two men started a war in a foreign country. It isn't the first time.

If these were the motives that impelled Bush and Blair, what drove the more covert forces behind them? It's clear now – and was then, actually – that Iraq had nothing to do with al-Qaeda, which was after all the supposed target. But in the end a war in Iraq suited a lot of people, who were happy to actively promote it, or at least approve of it or, if nothing else, not disapprove.

It suited the Bushmen, with their certainty that the American way was the *right* way, and their desire to finish what the first Gulf War had started. It suited sections of the military, anxious to road-test new weaponry and tactics. It suited arms dealers and weapons companies. It suited the oilmen, because it offered control over the tap, and weakened OPEC and the Saudis correspondingly. It suited the Israeli Right, so disproportionately represented in the White House, to have a potential enemy neutralized, and at the same time to send the strongest of signals to other "rogue states" in the region. It suited the Evangelical Christians, who saw this war as a step on the road to Rapture. It suited the Evangelical Democratizers, who thought that free-market capitalist democracy could be planted anywhere, anytime, and that things would certainly be better if it were. It suited the oil-hungry American economy, which saw the chance of global hegemony and wanted a big army in the Middle East, from there to keep an eye on things. It suited the ideal- ists – and there were many – who regarded Saddam as a monster who had to be removed (but unfortunately didn't ask the question "And then what?"). And it suited Tony Blair, perhaps for some of the obvious reasons, but perhaps mostly because he wanted to be leading from the front with his hero-pal, two crusad- ers for freedom. And it suited the hollow men and straw men – the apparatchiks of Blair's government – because, beyond anything else, they are people weak in mind and spirit who just want to be on the team that's winning.

9/11 had made the public scared enough, the media uncritical enough, and the politicians cowed enough for both the British and the American governments to rebrand the "War On Terror" as a war on Iraq. Both our governments knew there was no link between 9/11 and Iraq. They knew (from eight years of inspections and ten years of bombing and sanctions) that Iraq was not actually developing chemical, biological or nuclear weapons and that the regime was toothless and utterly unable to defend itself against the biggest attack in history by the biggest military power in history.

So in the end you can't help thinking that Iraq was invaded not because it was dangerous, as we claimed, but because it was the *least* threatening country in the region, and therefore the best place from which to begin a conquest of the Middle East. As Neo-Con and PNAC-man Ken Adelman predicted so confidently, and so wrongly, it would be a "cakewalk" – over in a few weeks.

The war wasn't over in a few weeks, and, in terms of any of its originally stated goals, has so far been a shattering failure. If it was meant to improve the lives of the Iraqi people, it failed. If it was meant to stem the tide of terrorism, it failed. If it was meant to make the world safer for the rest of us, it failed. If it was intended to stabilize the price of oil, it failed. If it was meant to be a "beacon of democracy" for the rest of the Arab world, it failed.

For the truth is that – along with their allies Berlusconi in Italy and Howard in Australia – Bush and Blair seem quite indifferent to actual democracy. It's a useful banner to fly above their ambitions – as though it's fine to destroy a country and several thousand of its people if, at the end of it, you can paste the label "DEMOCRACY" over the mess you've left.

The war has achieved one thing though. It has projected Western military power into new corners of the globe. Perhaps, for the backroom boys in the American government, this was the real ambition all along. America got what it wanted in Iraq and Afghanistan: 14 large military bases in the Middle East, lots of jobs for the boys, and a way of justifying to a stupefied population an ever-increasing military budget and ever-decreasing personal freedoms. And Britain was a useful muggins, eagerly following behind, the playground bully's brainy mate.

In fact militarily, the UK's presence in Iraq is almost irrelevant: we have 8,000 soldiers there compared to 160,000 Americans and an estimated 30,000 western mercenaries. Britain therefore represents under 5 per cent of the fighting force. But to the American government, Britain's support is crucial for quite another reason: it validates US actions, and reframes their strategic ambitions as part of a rational, international, democratic project. Without the UK, this war would appear as it really is: not "The West" against "Militant Islam," but the American superpower trying to conquer the Middle East.

And this is perhaps the most compelling reason for withdrawing our troops now. As long as we stay, we tell the rest of the world that we endorse this unnecessary and loathsome war, that we support this corrupt administration and its colonialist project. And we tell the world, that, with all our economic and scientific and cultural power, this is what we choose to do – to tyrannize and maim an already suffering country, in order, we say retrospectively, to free it from tyranny.

It is essential that we restore our standing in the world by making it clear that we, the British public, do not and never did support this insane project, and that we were the victims of a calculated program of propaganda and deceit by our government. And we must hold Blair and his gang to account for that – by impeaching him and by throwing them out.

For beyond the disaster of this vanity project there is an even bigger one. This war has so far cost *at least* 200 billion dollars. By UN estimates, for that amount we could have provided clean water for the 2 billion people who don't now have it – millions of whom will die from waterborne diseases. We could also have eradicated malaria – the world's most lethal disease – from the planet. And we could have provided the retroviral drugs that the world's AIDS victims need to stay alive. And there would have been cash left over to tackle a couple of other global problems. Perhaps we would have even started thinking about the biggest problem of all: climate change.

There are *real* problems in this world, problems that will need enormous vision and ingenuity and gen- erosity for their solution. The war in Iraq represents the lack of any of these, and the abject squandering of our potential as a civilization. We should be ashamed: not only for what we've done in Iraq, but for everything else we've thus failed to do.

JOHN LE CARRÉ

The United States Has Gone Mad

This article was written in January 2003: two months before the UN refused to authorize Bush and Blair's projected invasion of Iraq. The United Nations had become a focus for the hopes of many opponents of the war. Yet in June 2004, the UN went on to endorse the occupation of Iraq in Resolution 1546. The Pentagon has now rebranded the War on Terror as the Long War, and America appears to be setting its sights on Iran. While the media recites mantras about spreading freedom and democracy in the Middle East, Washington continues to condemn those countries – Palestine, Venezuela, Iran – that elect anyone other than the US's preferred candidate. The United States is descending further into madness, unchecked by either the constitution or the electorate. In Britain, for as long as we have Tony Blair singing the same lies as George Bush, America's hallucinations and nightmares will be ours.

AMERICA HAS entered one of its periods of historical madness, but this is the worst I can remember: worse than McCarthyism, worse than the Bay of Pigs and in the long term potentially more disastrous than the Vietnam War.

The reaction to 9/11 is beyond anything Osama bin Laden could have hoped for in his nastiest dreams. As in McCarthy times, the freedoms that have made America the envy of the world are being systematically eroded. The combination of compliant US media and vested corporate interests is once more ensuring that a debate that should be ringing out in every town square is confined to the loftier columns of the East Coast press.

The imminent war was planned years before bin Laden struck, but it was he who made it possible. Without bin Laden, the Bush junta would still be trying to explain such tricky matters as how it came to be elected in the first place; Enron; its shameless favouring of the already-too-rich; its reckless disregard for the world's poor, the ecology and a raft of unilaterally abrogated international treaties. They might also have to be telling us why they support Israel in its continuing disregard for UN resolutions.

But bin Laden conveniently swept all that under the carpet. The Bushies are riding high. Now 88 per cent of Americans want the war, we are told. The US defence budget has been raised by another $60 billion to around $360 billion. A splendid new generation of nuclear weapons is in the pipeline, so we can all breathe easy. Quite what war 88 per cent of Americans think they are supporting is a lot less clear. A war for how long, please? At what cost in American lives? At what cost to the American taxpayer's pocket? At what cost – because most of those 88 per cent are thoroughly decent and humane people – in Iraqi lives?

How Bush and his junta succeeded in deflecting America's anger from bin Laden to Saddam Hussein is one of the great public-relations conjuring tricks of history. But they swung it. A recent poll tells us that one in two Americans now believe Saddam was responsible for the attack on the World Trade Center. But the American public is not merely being misled. It is being browbeaten and kept in a state of ignorance and fear. The carefully orchestrated neurosis should carry Bush and his fellow conspirators nicely into the next election.

Those who are not with Mr Bush are against him. Worse, they are with the enemy. Which is odd, because I'm dead against Bush, but I would love to see Saddam's downfall – just not on Bush's terms and not by his methods. And not under the banner of such outrageous hypocrisy. The religious cant that will send American troops into battle is perhaps the most sickening aspect of this surreal war-to-be. Bush has an arm-lock on God. And God has very particular political opinions. God appointed America to save the world in any way that suits America. God appointed Israel to be the nexus of America's Middle Eastern policy, and anyone who wants to mess with that idea is a) anti-Semitic, b) anti-American, c) with the enemy, and d) a terrorist.

God also has pretty scary connections. In America, where all men are equal in His sight, if not in one another's, the Bush family numbers one President, one ex-President, one ex-head of the CIA, the Governor of Florida and the ex-Governor of Texas.

Care for a few pointers? George W. Bush, 1978–84: senior executive, Arbusto Energy/Bush Exploration, an oil company; 1986–90: senior executive of the Harken oil company. Dick Cheney, 1995–2000: chief executive of the Halliburton oil company. Condoleezza Rice, 1991–2000: senior executive with the Chevron oil company, which named an oil tanker after her. And so on. But none of these trifling associations affects the integrity of God's work.

In 1993, while ex-President George Bush was visiting the ever-democratic Kingdom of Kuwait to receive thanks for liberating them, somebody tried to kill him. The CIA believes that "somebody" was Saddam. Hence Bush Jr's cry: "That man tried to kill my Daddy." But it's still not personal, this war. It's still necessary. It's still God's work. It's still about bringing freedom and democracy to oppressed Iraqi people.

To be a member of the team you must also believe in Absolute Good and Absolute Evil, and Bush, with a lot of help from his friends, family and God, is there to tell us which is which. What Bush won't tell us is the truth about why we're going to war. What is at stake is not an Axis of Evil – but oil, money and people's lives. Saddam's misfortune is to sit on the second biggest oilfield in the world. Bush wants it, and who helps him get it will receive a piece of the cake. And who doesn't, won't.

If Saddam didn't have the oil, he could torture his citizens to his heart's content. Other leaders do it every day – think Saudi Arabia, think Pakistan, think Turkey, think Syria, think Egypt.

Baghdad represents no clear and present danger to its neighbours, and none to the US or Britain. Saddam's weapons of mass destruction, if he's still got them, will be peanuts by comparison with the stuff Israel or America could hurl at him at five minutes' notice. What is at stake is not an imminent military or terrorist threat, but the economic imperative of US growth. What is at stake is America's need to demonstrate its military power to all of us – to Europe and Russia and China, and poor mad little North Korea, as well as the Middle East; to show who rules America at home, and who is to be ruled by America abroad.

The most charitable interpretation of Tony Blair's part in all this is that he believed that, by riding the tiger, he could steer it. He can't. Instead, he gave it a phoney legitimacy, and a smooth voice. Now I fear, the same tiger has him penned into a corner, and he can't get out.

It is utterly laughable that, at a time when Blair has talked himself against the ropes, neither of Britain's opposition leaders can lay a glove on him. But that's Britain's tragedy, as it is America's: as our Governments spin, lie and lose their credibility, the electorate simply shrugs and looks the other way. Blair's best chance of personal survival must be that, at the eleventh hour, world protest and an improbably emboldened UN will force Bush to put his gun back in his holster unfired. But what happens when the world's greatest cowboy rides back into town without a tyrant's head to wave at the boys?

Blair's worst chance is that, with or without the UN, he will drag us into a war that, if the will to negotiate energetically had ever been there, could have been avoided; a war that has been no more democratically debated in Britain than it has in America or at the UN. By doing so, Blair will have set back our relations with Europe and the Middle East for decades to come. He will have helped to provoke unforeseeable retaliation, great domestic unrest, and regional chaos in the Middle East. Welcome to the party of the ethical foreign policy.

There is a middle way, but it's a tough one: Bush dives in without UN approval and Blair stays on the bank. Goodbye to the special relationship.

I cringe when I hear my Prime Minister lend his head prefect's sophistries to this colonialist adventure. His very real anxieties about terror are shared by all sane men. What he can't explain is how he reconciles a global assault on al-Qaeda with a territorial assault on Iraq. We are in this war, if it takes place, to secure the fig leaf of our special relationship, to grab our share of the oil pot, and because, after all the public hand-holding in Washington and Camp David, Blair has to show up at the altar.

"But will we win, Daddy?"

"Of course, child. It will all be over while you're still in bed."

"Why?"

"Because otherwise Mr Bush's voters will get terribly impatient and may decide not to vote for him."

"But will people be killed, Daddy?"

"Nobody you know, darling. Just foreign people."

"Can I watch it on television?"

"Only if Mr Bush says you can."

"And afterwards, will everything be normal again? Nobody will do anything horrid any more?"

"Hush child, and go to sleep."

Last Friday a friend of mine in California drove to his local supermarket with a sticker on his car saying: "Peace is also Patriotic." It was gone by the time he'd finished shopping.

HAROLD PINTER

Art, Truth and Politics

"THERE ARE no hard distinctions between what is real and what is unreal, nor between what is true and what is false. A thing is not necessarily either true or false; it can be both true and false."

I believe that these assertions still make sense and do still apply to the exploration of reality through art. So as a writer I stand by them but as a citizen I cannot. As a citizen I must ask: What is true? What is false?

Truth in drama is forever elusive. You never quite find it but the search for it is compulsive. The search is clearly what drives the endeavour. The search is your task. More often than not you stumble upon the truth in the dark, colliding with it or just glimpsing an image or a shape which seems to correspond to the truth, often without realising that you have done so. But the real truth is that there never is any such thing as one truth to be found in dramatic art. There are many. These truths challenge each other, recoil from each other, reflect each other, ignore each other, tease each other, are blind to each other. Sometimes you feel you have the truth of a moment in your hand, then it slips through your fingers and is lost.

I have often been asked how my plays come about. I cannot say. Nor can I ever sum up my plays, except to say that this is what happened. That is what they said. That is what they did.

Most of the plays are engendered by a line, a word or an image. The given word is often shortly followed by the image. I shall give two examples of two lines which came right out of the blue into my head, followed by an image, followed by me.

The plays are The Homecoming and Old Times. The first line of The Homecoming is "What have you done with the scissors?" The first line of Old Times is "Dark."

In each case I had no further information.

In the first case someone was obviously looking for a pair of scissors and was demanding their whereabouts of someone else he suspected had probably stolen them. But I somehow knew that the person addressed didn't give a damn about the scissors or about the questioner either, for that matter.

"Dark" I took to be a description of someone's hair, the hair of a woman, and was the answer to a question. In each case I found myself compelled to pursue the matter. This happened visually, a very slow fade, through shadow into light.

I always start a play by calling the characters A, B and C.

In the play that became The Homecoming I saw a man enter a stark room and ask his question of a younger man sitting on an ugly sofa reading a racing paper. I somehow suspected that A was a father and that B was his son, but I had no proof. This was however confirmed a short time later when B (later to become Lenny) says to A (later to become Max), "Dad, do you mind if I change the subject? I want to ask you something. The dinner we had before, what was the name of it? What do you call it? Why don't you buy a dog? You're a dog cook. Honest. You think you're cooking for a lot of dogs." So since B calls A "Dad" it seemed to me reasonable to assume that they were father and son. A was also clearly the cook and his cooking did not seem to be held in high regard. Did this mean that there was no mother? I didn't know. But, as I told myself at the time, our beginnings never know our ends.

"Dark." A large window. Evening sky. A man, A (later to become Deeley), and a woman, B (later to become Kate), sitting with drinks. "Fat or thin?" the man asks.

Who are they talking about? But I then see, standing at the window, a woman, C (later to become Anna), in another condition of light, her back to them, her hair dark.

It's a strange moment, the moment of creating characters who up to that moment have had no existence. What follows is fitful, uncertain, even hallucinatory, although sometimes it can be an unstoppable avalanche. The author's position is an odd one. In a sense he is not welcomed by the characters. The characters resist him, they are not easy to live with, they are impossible to define. You certainly can't dictate to them. To a certain extent you play a never-ending game with them, cat and mouse, blind man's buff, hide and seek. But finally you find that you have people of flesh and blood on your hands, people with will and an individual sensibility of their own, made out of component parts you are unable to change, manipulate or distort.

So language in art remains a highly ambiguous transaction, a quicksand, a trampoline, a frozen pool which might give way under you, the author, at any time.

But as I have said, the search for the truth can never stop. It cannot be adjourned, it cannot be postponed. It has to be faced, right there, on the spot.

Political theatre presents an entirely different set of problems. Sermonizing has to be avoided at all cost. Objectivity is essential. The characters must be allowed to breathe their own air. The author cannot confine and constrict them to satisfy his own taste or disposition or prejudice. He must be prepared to approach them from a variety of angles, from a full and uninhibited range of perspectives, take them by surprise, perhaps, occasionally, but nevertheless give them the freedom to go which way they will. This does not always work. And political satire, of course, adheres to none of these precepts, in fact does precisely the opposite, which is its proper function.

In my play The Birthday Party I think I allow a whole range of options to operate in a dense forest of possibility before finally focussing on an act of subjugation.

Mountain Language pretends to no such range of operation. It remains brutal, short and ugly. But the soldiers in the play do get some fun out of it. One sometimes forgets that torturers become easily bored. They need a bit of a laugh to keep their spirits up. This has been confirmed of course by the events at Abu Ghraib in Baghdad. Mountain Language lasts only 20 minutes, but it could go on for hour after hour, on and on and on, the same pattern repeated over and over again, on and on, hour after hour.

Ashes to Ashes, on the other hand, seems to me to be taking place under water. A drowning woman, her hand reaching up through the waves, dropping down out of sight, reaching for others, but finding nobody there, either above or under the water, finding only shadows, reflections, floating; the woman a lost figure in a drowning landscape, a woman unable to escape the doom that seemed to belong only to others.

But as they died, she must die too.

Political language, as used by politicians, does not venture into any of this territory since the majority of politicians, on the evidence available to us, are interested not in truth but in power and in the maintenance of that power. To maintain that power it is essential that people remain in ignorance, that they live in ignorance of the truth, even the truth of their own lives. What surrounds us therefore is a vast tapestry of lies, upon which we feed.

As every single person here knows, the justification for the invasion of Iraq was that Saddam Hussein possessed a highly dangerous body of weapons of mass destruction, some of which could be fired in 45 minutes, bringing about appalling devastation. We were assured that was true. It was not true. We were told that Iraq had a relationship with al-Qaeda and shared responsibility for the atrocity in New York of September 11 2001. We were assured that this was true. It was not true. We were told that Iraq threatened the security of the world. We were assured it was true. It was not true.

The truth is something entirely different. The truth is to do with how the United States understands its role in the world and how it chooses to embody it.

But before I come back to the present I would like to look at the recent past, by which I mean United States foreign policy since the end of the Second World War. I believe it is obligatory upon us to subject this period to at least some kind of even limited scrutiny, which is all that time will allow here.

Everyone knows what happened in the Soviet Union and throughout Eastern Europe during the post-war period: the systematic brutality, the widespread atrocities, the ruthless suppression of independent thought. All this has been fully documented and verified.

But my contention here is that the US crimes in the same period have only been superficially recorded, let alone documented, let alone acknowledged, let alone recognized as crimes at all. I believe this must be addressed and that the truth has considerable bearing on where the world stands now. Although constrained, to a certain extent, by the existence of the Soviet Union, the United States' actions throughout the world made it clear that it had concluded it had carte blanche to do what it liked.

Direct invasion of a sovereign state has never in fact been America's favoured method. In the main, it has preferred what it has described as "low intensity conflict." Low intensity conflict means that thousands of people die but slower than if you dropped a bomb on them in one fell swoop. It means that you infect the heart of the country, that you establish a malignant growth and watch the gangrene bloom. When the populace has been subdued – or beaten to death – the same thing – and your own friends, the military and the great corporations, sit comfortably in power, you go before the camera and say that democracy has prevailed. This was a commonplace in US foreign policy in the years to which I refer.

The tragedy of Nicaragua was a highly significant case. I choose to offer it here as a potent example of America's view of its role in the world, both then and now.

I was present at a meeting at the US embassy in London in the late 1980s.

The United States Congress was about to decide whether to give more money to the Contras in their campaign against the state of Nicaragua. I was a member of a delegation speaking on behalf of Nicaragua but the most important member of this delegation was a Father John Metcalf. The leader of the US body was Raymond Seitz (then number two to the ambassador, later ambassador himself). Father Metcalf said: "Sir, I am in charge of a parish in the north of Nicaragua. My parishioners built a school, a health centre, a cultural centre. We have lived in peace. A few months ago a Contra force attacked the parish. They destroyed everything: the school, the health centre, the cultural centre. They raped nurses and teachers, slaughtered doctors, in the most brutal manner. They behaved like savages. Please demand that the US government withdraw its support from this shocking terrorist activity."

Raymond Seitz had a very good reputation as a rational, responsible and highly sophisticated man. He was greatly respected in diplomatic circles. He listened, paused and then spoke with some gravity. "Father," he said, "let me tell you something. In war, innocent people always suffer." There was a frozen silence. We stared at him. He did not flinch.

Innocent people, indeed, always suffer.

Finally somebody said: "But in this case 'innocent people' were the victims of a gruesome atrocity subsidized by your government, one among many. If Congress allows the Contras more money further atrocities of this kind will take place. Is this not the case? Is your government not therefore guilty of supporting acts of murder and destruction upon the citizens of a sovereign state?"

Seitz was imperturbable. "I don't agree that the facts as presented support your assertions," he said.

As we were leaving the Embassy a US aide told me that he enjoyed my plays. I did not reply.

I should remind you that at the time President Reagan made the following statement: "The Contras are the moral equivalent of our Founding Fathers."

The United States supported the brutal Somoza dictatorship in Nicaragua for over 40 years. The Nicaraguan people, led by the Sandinistas, overthrew this regime in 1979, a breathtaking popular revolution.

The Sandinistas weren't perfect. They possessed their fair share of arrogance and their political philosophy contained a number of contradictory elements. But they were intelligent, rational and civilized. They set out to establish a stable, decent, pluralistic society. The death penalty was abolished. Hundreds of thousands of poverty-stricken peasants were brought back from the dead. Over 100,000 families were given title to land. Two thousand schools were built. A quite remarkable literacy campaign reduced illiteracy in the country to less than one seventh. Free education was established and a free health service. Infant mortality was reduced by a third. Polio was eradicated.

The United States denounced these achievements as Marxist/Leninist subversion. In the view of the US government, a dangerous example was being set. If Nicaragua was allowed to establish basic norms of social and economic justice, if it was allowed to raise the standards of health care and education and achieve social unity and national self respect, neighbouring countries would ask the same questions and do the same things. There was of course at the time fierce resistance to the status quo in El Salvador.

I spoke earlier about "a tapestry of lies" which surrounds us. President Reagan commonly described Nicaragua as a "totalitarian dungeon." This was taken generally by the media, and certainly by the British government, as accurate and fair comment. But there was in fact no record of death squads under the Sandinista government. There was no record of torture. There was no record of systematic or official military brutality. No priests were ever murdered in Nicaragua. There were in fact three priests in the government, two Jesuits and a Maryknoll missionary. The totalitarian dungeons were actually next door, in El Salvador and Guatemala. The United States had brought down the democratically elected government of Guatemala in 1954 and it is estimated that over 200,000 people had been victims of successive military dictatorships.

Six of the most distinguished Jesuits in the world were viciously murdered at the Central American University in San Salvador in 1989 by a battalion of the Alcatl regiment trained at Fort Benning, Georgia, USA. That extremely brave man Archbishop Romero was assassinated while saying mass. It is estimated that 75,000 people died. Why were they killed? They were killed because they believed a better life was possible and should be achieved. That belief immediately qualified them as communists. They died because they dared to question the status quo, the endless plateau of poverty, disease, degradation and oppression, which had been their birthright.

The United States finally brought down the Sandinista government. It took some years and considerable resistance but relentless economic persecution and 30,000 dead finally undermined the spirit of the Nicaraguan people. They were exhausted and poverty stricken once again. The casinos moved back into the country. Free health and free education were over. Big business returned with a vengeance. "Democracy" had prevailed.

But this "policy" was by no means restricted to Central America. It was conducted throughout the world. It was never-ending. And it is as if it never happened.

The United States supported and in many cases engendered every right-wing military dictatorship in the world after the end of the Second World War. I refer to Indonesia, Greece, Uruguay, Brazil, Paraguay, Haiti, Turkey, the Philippines, Guatemala, El Salvador, and, of course, Chile. The horror the United States inflicted upon Chile in 1973 can never be purged and can never be forgiven.

Hundreds of thousands of deaths took place throughout these countries. Did they take place? And are they in all cases attributable to US foreign policy? The answer is yes they did take place and they are attributable to American foreign policy. But you wouldn't know it.

It never happened. Nothing ever happened. Even while it was happening it wasn't happening. It didn't matter. It was of no interest. The crimes of the United States have been systematic, constant, vicious, remorseless, but very few people have actually talked about them. You have to hand it to America. It has exercised a quite clinical manipulation of power worldwide while masquerading as a force for universal good. It's a brilliant, even witty, highly successful act of hypnosis.

I put to you that the United States is without doubt the greatest show on the road. Brutal, indifferent, scornful and ruthless it may be but it is also very clever. As a salesman it is out on its own and its most saleable commodity is self love. It's a winner. Listen to all American presidents on television say the words, "the American people," as in the sentence, "I say to the American people it is time to pray and to defend the rights of the American people and I ask the American people to trust their president in the action he is about to take on behalf of the American people."

It's a scintillating stratagem. Language is actually employed to keep thought at bay. The words "the American people" provide a truly voluptuous cushion of reassurance. You don't need to think. Just lie back on the cushion. The cushion may be suffocating your intelligence and your critical faculties but it's very comfortable. This does not apply of course to the 40 million people living below the poverty line and the 2 million men and women imprisoned in the vast gulag of prisons, which extends across the US.

The United States no longer bothers about low intensity conflict. It no longer sees any point in being reticent or even devious. It puts its cards on the table without fear or favour. It quite simply doesn't give a damn about the United Nations, international law or critical dissent, which it regards as impotent and irrelevant. It also has its own bleating little lamb tagging behind it on a lead, the pathetic and supine Great Britain.

What has happened to our moral sensibility? Did we ever have any? What do these words mean? Do they refer to a term very rarely employed these days – conscience? A conscience to do not only with our own acts but to do with our shared responsibility in the acts of others? Is all this dead? Look at Guantanamo Bay. Hundreds of people detained without charge for over three years, with no legal representation or due process, technically detained forever. This totally illegitimate structure is maintained in defiance of the Geneva Convention. It is not only tolerated but hardly thought about by what's called the "international community." This criminal outrage is being committed by a country which declares itself to be "the leader of the free world." Do we think about the inhabitants of Guantanamo Bay? What does the media say about them? They pop up occasionally – a small item on page six. They have been consigned to a no man's land from which indeed they may never return. At present many are on hunger strike, being force-fed, including British residents. No niceties in these force-feeding procedures. No sedative or anaesthetic. Just a tube stuck up your nose and into your throat. You vomit blood. This is torture. What has the British Foreign Secretary said about this? Nothing. What has the British Prime Minister said about this? Nothing. Why not? Because the United States has said: to criticize our conduct in Guantanamo Bay constitutes an unfriendly act. You're either with us or against us. So Blair shuts up.

The invasion of Iraq was a bandit act, an act of blatant state terrorism, demonstrating absolute contempt for the concept of international law. The invasion was an arbitrary military action inspired by a series of lies upon lies and gross manipulation of the media and therefore of the public; an act intended to consolidate American military and economic control of the

Middle East masquerading – as a last resort – all other justifications having failed to justify themselves – as liberation. A formidable assertion of military force responsible for the death and mutilation of thousands and thousands of innocent people.

We have brought torture, cluster bombs, depleted uranium, innumerable acts of random murder, misery, degradation and death to the Iraqi people and call it "bringing freedom and democracy to the Middle East."

How many people do you have to kill before you qualify to be described as a mass murderer and a war criminal? One hundred thousand? More than enough, I would have thought. Therefore it is just that Bush and Blair be arraigned before the International Criminal Court of Justice. But Bush has been clever. He has not ratified the International Criminal Court of Justice. Therefore if any American soldier or for that matter politician finds himself in the dock Bush has warned that he will send in the marines. But Tony Blair has ratified the Court and is therefore available for prosecution. We can let the Court have his address if they're interested. It is Number 10, Downing Street, London.

Death in this context is irrelevant. Both Bush and Blair place death well away on the back burner. At least 100,000 Iraqis were killed by American bombs and missiles before the Iraq insurgency began. These people are of no moment. Their deaths don't exist. They are blank. They are not even recorded as being dead. "We don't do body counts," said the American general Tommy Franks.

Early in the invasion there was a photograph published on the front page of British newspapers of Tony Blair kissing the cheek of a little Iraqi boy. "A grateful child," said the caption. A few days later there was a story and photograph, on an inside page, of another four-year-old boy with no arms. His family had been blown up by a missile. He was the only survivor. "When do I get my arms back?" he asked. The story was dropped. Well, Tony Blair wasn't holding him in his arms, nor the body of any other mutilated child, nor the body of any bloody corpse. Blood is dirty. It dirties your shirt and tie when you're making a sincere speech on television.

The 2,000 American dead are an embarrassment. They are transported to their graves in the dark. Funerals are unobtrusive, out of harm's way. The mutilated rot in their beds, some for the rest of their lives. So the dead and the mutilated both rot, in different kinds of graves.

Here is an extract from a poem by Pablo Neruda, "I'm Explaining a Few Things":

> And one morning all that was burning,
> one morning the bonfires

leapt out of the earth
devouring human beings
and from then on fire,
gunpowder from then on,
and from then on blood.
Bandits with planes and Moors,
bandits with finger-rings and duchesses,
bandits with black friars spattering blessings
came through the sky to kill children
and the blood of children ran through the streets
without fuss, like children's blood.
Jackals that the jackals would despise
stones that the dry thistle would bite on and spit out,
vipers that the vipers would abominate.
Face to face with you I have seen the blood
of Spain tower like a tide
to drown you in one wave
of pride and knives.
Treacherous
generals:
see my dead house,
look at broken Spain:
from every house burning metal flows
instead of flowers
from every socket of Spain
Spain emerges
and from every dead child a rifle with eyes
and from every crime bullets are born
which will one day find
the bull's eye of your hearts.
And you will ask: why doesn't his poetry
speak of dreams and leaves
and the great volcanoes of his native land.
Come and see the blood in the streets.

Come and see
the blood in the streets.
Come and see the blood
in the streets!

Let me make it quite clear that in quoting from
Neruda's poem I am in no way comparing Republican
Spain to Saddam Hussein's Iraq. I quote Neruda
because nowhere in contemporary poetry have I read
such a powerful visceral description of the bombing
of civilians.

I have said earlier that the United States is now
totally frank about putting its cards on the table. That
is the case. Its official declared policy is now defined as
"full spectrum dominance." That is not my term, it is
theirs. "Full spectrum dominance" means control of
land, sea, air and space and all attendant resources.

The United States now occupies 702 military
installations throughout the world in 132 countries,
with the honourable exception of Sweden, of course.
We don't quite know how they got there but they are
there all right.

The United States possesses 8,000 active and
operational nuclear warheads. Two thousand are
on hair trigger alert, ready to be launched with 15
minutes' warning. It is developing new systems of
nuclear force, known as bunker busters. The British,
ever cooperative, are intending to replace their own

nuclear missile, Trident. Who, I wonder, are they aiming at? Osama bin Laden? You? Me? Joe Dokes? China? Paris? Who knows? What we do know is that this infantile insanity – the possession and threatened use of nuclear weapons – is at the heart of present American political philosophy. We must remind ourselves that the United States is on a permanent military footing and shows no sign of relaxing it.

Many thousands, if not millions, of people in the United States itself are demonstrably sickened, shamed and angered by their government's actions, but as things stand they are not a coherent political force – yet. But the anxiety, uncertainty and fear which we can see growing daily in the United States is unlikely to diminish.

I know that President Bush has many extremely competent speech writers but I would like to volunteer for the job myself. I propose the following short address which he can make on television to the nation. I see him grave, hair carefully combed, serious, winning, sincere, often beguiling, sometimes employing a wry smile, curiously attractive, a man's man.

"God is good. God is great. God is good. My God is good. Bin Laden's God is bad. His is a bad God. Saddam's God was bad, except he didn't have one. He was a barbarian. We are not barbarians. We don't chop people's heads off. We believe in freedom. So does God. I am not a barbarian. I am the democratically elected leader of a freedom-loving democracy. We are a compassionate society. We give compassionate electrocution and compassionate lethal injection. We are a great nation. I am not a dictator. He is. I am not a barbarian. He is. And he is. They all are. I possess moral authority. You see this fist? This is my moral authority. And don't you forget it."

A writer's life is a highly vulnerable, almost naked activity. We don't have to weep about that. The writer makes his choice and is stuck with it. But it is true to say that you are open to all the winds, some of them icy indeed. You are out on your own, out on a limb. You find no shelter, no protection – unless you lie – in which case of course you have constructed your own protection and, it could be argued, become a politician.

I have referred to death quite a few times this evening. I shall now quote a poem of my own called "Death."

> Where was the dead body found?
> Who found the dead body?
> Was the dead body dead when found?
> How was the dead body found?
> Who was the dead body?
> Who was the father or daughter or brother
> Or uncle or sister or mother or son
> Of the dead and abandoned body?
> Was the body dead when abandoned?

Was the body abandoned?
By whom had it been abandoned?
Was the dead body naked or dressed for a journey?
What made you declare the dead body dead?
Did you declare the dead body dead?
How well did you know the dead body?
How did you know the dead body was dead?
Did you wash the dead body
Did you close both its eyes
Did you bury the body
Did you leave it abandoned
Did you kiss the dead body

When we look into a mirror we think the image that confronts us is accurate. But move a millimetre and the image changes. We are actually looking at a never-ending range of reflections. But sometimes a writer has to smash the mirror – for it is on the other side of that mirror that the truth stares at us.

I believe that despite the enormous odds which exist, unflinching, unswerving, fierce intellectual determination, as citizens, to define the real truth of our lives and our societies is a crucial obligation which devolves upon us all. It is in fact mandatory.

If such a determination is not embodied in our political vision we have no hope of restoring what is so nearly lost to us – the dignity of man.

RICHARD DAWKINS

Bin Laden's Victory

I wrote this article on March 18 2003, two days before Iraq was invaded. This is the first time that the original version has been published in full, and I have deliberately refrained from using hindsight to change it. Re-reading it now, I can see that I overestimated the permanence of the rifts in Europe, NATO and the UN. But I got the effect on Iraq itself and the Muslim world exactly right, and my hypothetical soliloquy by Osama bin Laden need in no way be modified. My innuendo that no weapons of mass destruction would be found has proved correct – but that was not a difficult prediction to make. Blair and Bush still insist that they were honestly mistaken and acting on the best intelligence available at the time. But Hans Blix's investigation was proceeding apace, and was showing every indication that no weapons would turn up. Given what we now know of Bush's eagerness to go to war come what may, and Blair's eagerness to please Bush come what may, I think that accusations of outright lying can fairly be made.

I WRITE this on the eve of war, haunted by W. H. Auden's lines on September 1, 1939:

> I sit in one of the dives
> On fifty second street

Uncertain and afraid
As the clever hopes expire . . .

Whether this mad escapade will end sooner (as we all
must now hope) or later (as many of us fear), it will
not be the end. The Islamic world will in any case be
plunged into a seething stew of humiliated resent-
ment, from which generations of "martyrs" will rise,
led by new Osamas. The scars of enmity between
Britain and our erstwhile friends in Europe may take
years to heal. NATO may never recover. As for the UN,
quite apart from the corrupt spectacle of the world's
leading power bribing and bullying small countries
to hand over their votes, it is mortally wounded. The
fragile semblance of a rule-of-law in international
affairs, painstakingly built up since World War II,
is collapsing. A precedent is set for any country to
attack any other country it happens to dislike and is
strong enough to defeat. Who knows how this precedent may play itself out, if followed by North Korea,
Israel, Pakistan or India, countries which really *do*
have weapons of mass destruction?

Osama bin Laden, in his wildest dreams, could
hardly have hoped for this. A mere eighteen months
after he boosted the United States to a peak of worldwide sympathy and popularity unprecedented since
Pearl Harbor, the totality of that international good-
will has been squandered to near zero. Bin Laden must

be beside himself with glee. And, Allah be praised, the infidels are now walking right into the Iraq trap.

There was always a risk for bin Laden that his attacks on New York and Washington might raise world sympathy for the United States, thereby thwarting his long-term aim of holy war against the Great Satan. He needn't have worried. With the Bush junta at the helm, a camel could have foreseen the outcome. And the beauty is that it doesn't matter what happens in the war. Imagine how it looks from bin Laden's warped point of view:

If the American victory is swift, Bush will have done our work for us, removing the hated Saddam Hussein with his secular, un-Islamic ways, and opening the way for a decent theocracy ruled by Ayatollahs or Talibans. Even better, as a war "hero" the strutting, swaggering Bush may actually win an election. Who can guess what he will then get up to, and what resentments he will arouse, when he finally has something to swagger about? We shall have so many martyrs volunteering, we shall run out of targets. Or, if the American victory is slow and bloody, things might be better still. Admittedly, Bush will probably fall in 2004 and Saddam be seen as a martyr, but never mind. The hatred that a prolonged war generates will set us up for the foreseeable future, even if the Americans elect a less gloriously useful President. How could we have hoped for more?

A handful of the zealous faithful, mostly Saudis with a few Egyptians, armed only with box-cutters and deep religious faith, simultaneously commandeered four large airliners and flew three of them, undisturbed by fighter aircraft or – mysteriously – by any immediate government attention at all, into large buildings with catastrophic loss of life. Praise be to Allah. But mark the sequel. It is almost too good to be true but, as a direct consequence of this attack, the entire might of the United States Army, Navy and Air Force is diverted away from us, and hurled at a completely different country, whose only connection with 9/11 is that its people belong to the same "race" and religion as our glorious martyrs.

The claim that this war is about "weapons of mass destruction" is either dishonest or betrays a lack of foresight verging on negligence. Why was it not a central plank in the platforms of George Bush and Tony Blair in their respective election campaigns? Neither of them mentioned the war. The only major leader who has an electoral mandate for his war policy is the German chancellor Gerhard Schröder – and he is against it. Why did Bush, with Blair trotting dutifully to heel, suddenly start threatening to invade Iraq when he did, and not before? The answer is embarrassingly obvious. Illogical though it undoubtedly is, everything changed on September 11.

Whatever anyone may say about weapons of mass destruction, or about Saddam's savage brutality to his own people, the reason Bush can now get away with his lovely war is that a sufficient number of Americans (including, incredibly, even Bush himself to judge from his recent address to the nation) see it as *revenge* for 9/11. This is worse than bizarre. It is pure racism and/or religious prejudice, given that nobody has made even a faintly plausible case that Iraq had anything to do with the atrocity. It was Arabs that hit the World Trade Center, right? So let's go kick Arab ass. Those 9/11 terrorists were Muslims, right? Right. And Iraqis are Muslims, right? Right. That does it.

Bush seems sincerely to see the world as a battle-ground between Good and Evil (the capital letters are deliberate). It is Us against Them, St Michael's angels against the forces of Lucifer. We're gonna smoke out the Amalekites, send a posse after the Midianites, smite them all and let God sort out their souls. Minds doped up on this kind of Good versus Evil cod-theology have a hard time distinguishing between Saddam Hussein and Osama bin Laden. Some of Bush's faithful supporters even welcome war as the necessary prelude to the final showdown between Good and Evil: Armageddon followed by the Rapture. We must presume, or at least hope, that Bush himself is not quite of that bonkers persuasion. But he really does seem to believe he is wrestling, on God's behalf, against some sort of disembodied spirit of Evil. Tony Blair is, of course, far more intelligent and able than Bush. But his unshakeable conviction that he is right and almost everybody else wrong does have a certain theological feel. He denied Jeremy Paxman's wickedly funny suggestion that he and Dubya pray together, but does "Reverend Blair," too, believe in Evil?

Like "sin" (which I was taught was responsible for all disease in the world) and like "terror" (Bush's favourite target before the current Iraq distraction) evil is not an entity, not a spirit, not a force to be opposed and subdued. Evil is a collection of nasty things that nasty people do. There are nasty people in every country, stupid people, insane people, people who, for all sorts of reasons, should never be allowed to get anywhere near power. Just killing nasty people doesn't help: they will simply be replaced. We must try to tailor our institutions, our constitutions, our electoral systems, so as to minimize the chance that they will rise to the top. In the case of Saddam Hussein, we in the west must bear some guilt. The United States, Britain and France have all, from time to time, done their bit to shore up Saddam and even arm him. And we democracies might look to our own vaunted institutions. Are they well designed to ensure that we don't make disastrous mistakes when we come to choose our own leaders? Isn't it, indeed, just such a mistake that has led us to this terrible pass today?

The population of the United States is nearly 300 million, including many of the best-educated, most talented, most resourceful, most ingenious, most humane people on earth. By almost any measure of civilized attainment, from Nobel Prize-counts on down, the United States leads the world by miles. You would think that a country with such resources, and such a field of talent, would be able to devise a constitution and an electoral procedure that would ensure a leadership of the highest quality. Yet, what has happened? At the end of all the Primaries and Party Caucuses, after all the speeches and the televised debates, after a year or more of non-stop electioneering bustle and balloons and razzamatazz, who, out of that entire population of 300 million, emerges at the top of the heap? George W Bush.

O my American friends, you know how much I love your country. Forgive my presumption, but could it just be that there is something a teeny weeny bit wrong with that famous constitution of yours? Yes, I admit that Mr Bush probably isn't as stupid as he sounds, and heaven knows he can't be as stupid as he looks. I admit that most of you didn't vote for him anyway, but that is part of my point. The system by which you elect your Presidents has been asking for trouble for years (and brother, have we now got trouble?).

Is it really, for example, a good idea that a single person's vote, buried deep within the margin of error for a whole State, can by itself swing a full 25 votes in the Electoral College, one way or the other? And is it really sensible that money should translate itself so directly and transparently into electoral success, so that a successful candidate must either be very rich or prepared to sell favours to those who are?

When a company seeks a new Chief Executive Officer, or a university a new Vice Chancellor, enormous trouble is taken to find the best person available. Professional headhunting firms may be engaged, written references are taken up and studied, exhaustive rounds of interviews are conducted, psychological aptitude tests are administered, confidential positive vetting may even be undertaken. Mistakes are still sometimes made, but it is not for want of strenuous efforts to avoid them. O my American friends, would you do business with a company that devoted an entire year to little else than the process of choosing its new CEO, from the strongest field in the world, and ended up with George W Bush?

Saddam Hussein has been a catastrophe for Iraq, but he never posed a threat outside his immediate neighbourhood. George W Bush is a catastrophe for the world. And a dream for Osama bin Laden.

HAIFA ZANGANA

The Right to Rule Ourselves

I N HIS last monthly press conference before the invasion of Iraq on February 18 2003, Prime Minister Tony Blair said that removing Saddam from power would "save a lot of lives," as well as eradicating Iraq's supposed chemical and biological weapons program. "The people who will celebrate the most will be the people of Iraq," Blair announced.

We are not celebrating. Death is covering us like fine dust.

These days, a familiar sight in Iraq is of shocked bystanders and shopkeepers collecting the scattered remains of bomb-blast victims for burial; another is of men hosing down pavements covered with their blood. Swift burial is kinder and cleaner than the stench of rapidly decomposing bodies piled up in morgues without electricity, waiting to be identified.

As in Britain, there were no suicide bombers in Iraq before the war. Now, they strike frequently. Why?

Despite all the rhetoric about "building a new democracy," Iraqis are buckling under the burden and abuses of the US-led occupation and its local Iraqi subcontractors.

Powerless, and with no credibility among Iraqi people, the successive interim governments have been a disaster. There is no security, and not the slightest improvement in electricity supply, availability of clean water, employment, or health and education services.

In a land awash with oil, 16 million Iraqis now rely on monthly food handouts for survival. Privatization threatens formerly free public services. Acute malnutrition among children has doubled. Unemployment, currently running at 60 per cent, has fuelled poverty, crime and prostitution. In government, corruption and nepotism are rampant.

Daily life for most Iraqis is still a struggle for survival. During the occupation human rights have proved, like weapons of mass destruction, to be a mirage. Torture and ill-treatment – even of children – is rife.

We have witnessed an escalation of Israeli-style "collective punishment" visited on Iraqi cities. On September 19 2004, during the siege of the northern town of Tell Afar, US troops cut off water and blocked food supplies to 150,000 refugees for three days. In Samarra, residents cowered in their homes as tanks and warplanes pounded the city. Bodies were strewn in the streets but could not be collected for fear of American snipers. Of the 130 Iraqis killed there, most were civilians. Hospital access was denied to the injured. In Falluja, on November 15 2004, NBC television captured the execution of a wounded Iraqi inside a mosque by a US Marine; this was one of many such murders, according to an eyewitness interviewed by Al-Jazeera television.

Our historical cities, our mosques, our houses have been desecrated, bombed time and again by US and UK warplanes. 500-pound bombs, cluster bombs, depleted uranium and banned weapons such as the MK-77 bomb – a modern form of napalm – have been used.

The photograph of an elderly Iraqi carrying a child's burned body in Falluja, taken during the November 2004 siege by US forces, is a carbon copy of another distressingly iconic image, from Halabja in March 1988. Both children were victims of chemical weapons: the first killed by a dictator who had no respect for democracy and human rights; the second by US troops, assisted by the British, operating under the respectable banner of "democracy" while showering Iraqis with white phosphorus and depleted uranium.

The Falluja photograph is emblematic of a racist occupation. We read in November 2005 that US troops were "stunned by what they found" during a raid on a ministry of the interior building: more than a hundred prisoners, many of whom "appeared to have been brutally beaten" and malnourished. There were also reports of dead bodies showing "signs of severe torture." Hussein Kamel, the deputy interior minister, was similarly "stunned." This feigned surprise is a farce. In the new dispensation, torture has continued unabated in detention centers, prisons, camps and secret cells. Abu Ghraib is merely the tip of the iceberg.

While the US and British governments have spent three years of occupation arguing for the legality of chemical weapons and the "usefulness" of torture to extract information, Iraqis have been engaged in a different struggle: to survive the increasingly brutal occupation, and to define democracy and human rights accordingly.

Instances of collective punishment, random arrest and murder are widespread. On October 16 2005, a group of adults and children gathered around a burnt-out Humvee on the edge of the town of Ramadi. There was a crater in the road, left by a bomb that had killed five US soldiers and two Iraqi soldiers the previous day. Some of the children were playing hide-and-seek, others laughing while pelting the vehicle with stones, when a US F-15 fighter jet roared overhead, firing on the crowd. The US military subsequently announced that it had killed 70 insurgents in air strikes, and knew of no civilian deaths. Among the "insurgents" killed that day were six-year-old Muhammad Salih Ali, who was buried in a plastic bag after relatives collected what they believed to be parts of his body; four-year-old Saad Ahmed Fuad; and his eight-year-old sister, Haifa, who had to be buried without one of her legs, as her family were unable to find it.

These and many other atrocities go unrecorded and unacknowledged. Amid a virtual mass media blackout in the UK, and an almost total lack of press freedom in Iraq, our dead have remained nameless, faceless. No US or British officials, or their proxies in the various Iraqi interim governments, have been willing to acknowledge our dead. How can they acknowledge the death of more than 100,000 civilians, most of them women and children, without being held responsible and accountable?

Most Iraqis are indifferent to the political timetable imposed by the occupiers – from the nominal "handover of sovereignty" to the bizarre three-month period of sectarian and ethnic wrangling about the interim government, and the excited declaration of a "yes" vote on the draft constitution by Condoleezza Rice within hours of the ballot boxes closing. Iraqis think the whole process is intended to divert their attention from the main issues: the occupation, the corruption, the pillaging of Iraq's resources, and the interim government's catastrophic failure on human rights.

A recent Human Rights Watch report gave fresh details of torture of prisoners by US forces in Iraq. At the Mercury military base near Falluja, abuse was not only overlooked, but encouraged and sometimes ordered. The report describes routine, severe beatings of prisoners, and the application of burning chemicals to detainees' eyes and skin, to make them glow in the dark. Throughout Iraq, thousands have been detained for months, sometimes years, without charge or trial, including the writer Muhsin al-Khafaji, who was arrested in May 2003 and remains in US custody in southern Iraq.

Women are taken as hostages by US soldiers to persuade fugitive male relatives to surrender or confess to terrorist acts. Sarah Taha al-Jumaily, 20, from Falluja, was arrested twice. On October 8, 2005, she was accused of being the daughter of Musab al-Zarqawi – despite the fact that US troops had already detained her father, a member of a pan-Arab party, for over two months. On October 19 she was arrested on suspicion of being a terrorist. Hundreds of people demonstrated, and workers went on strike to demand her release. The interior ministry states that 122 women remain in prison, charged with the novel crime of being "potential suicide bombers."

Iraqi journalists are frequently harassed, threatened and attacked by occupying troops. Since the US-led invasion 44 journalists and 6 Iraqi media workers have been killed. Many journalists have fled the country.

More than 100 Iraqi doctors and consultants have been killed or kidnapped in the past year. A spokesperson for the Iraqi Medical Society described the kidnappings as "intimidating and forcing them to leave the country."

Thousands of people are still missing. Their families endure an agonizing wait for word of the fate of their loved ones.

In a letter to a friend in Europe, Abdul Razaq al-Na'as, a Baghdad university professor in his 50s, grieved for his killed friends and colleagues. He concluded his letter: "I wonder who is next!"

He was.

At 2.45 pm, on Saturday January 28 2006, al Na'as drove away from his office at Baghdad University's College of Media. Two cars blocked his and gunmen opened fire, killing him instantly.

Al Na'as is not the first academic to be killed in the mayhem of the "new Iraq." Hundreds of academics and scientists have met this fate following the March 2003 invasion. Baghdad universities alone mourned the killing of over 80 members of their staff.

The minister of education stated recently that during 2005, 296 members of academic staff were killed and 133 wounded.

Not one of these crimes has been investigated by occupation forces or the interim governments. They leave this to international humanitarian organizations and anti-war movements. One such organization is the BRussells Tribunal on Iraq, which is attempting to compile a list with the information necessary to convince the special rapporteur on summary executions at UNHCHR in Geneva to investigate this matter; it does so with the help of Iraqi academics, who risk their lives in the process. Their research so far shows that the victims are men and women from all over Iraq, from different ethnic, religious and political backgrounds. Most of them are vocally opposed to the occupation. For the most part, they are killed in a fashion that suggests cold-blooded professional assassination. No-one has claimed responsibility.

Like many Iraqis, I believe these killings are politically motivated, related to the occupying forces' failure to gain any social support in the country. For the occupation to last, or for its aims to be fulfilled, independent minds have to be eradicated. We feel that we are witnessing a deliberate attempt to destroy intellectual life in Iraq.

Dr al Na'as was a familiar face on the Al-Jazeera and Al-Arabiya television stations. He had often condemned the continued presence of US-led troops in Iraq, and criticized the sectarian interim governments and their militias. His case echoes the assassination of Dr Abdullateef al Mayah, Director of the Centre of Arab studies at Baghdad's Mustansiriyah University. A prominent human-rights campaigner and critic of the occupation, Mayah was killed on the morning of January 19 2004 – only 12 hours after he had appeared on Al-Jazeera denouncing the corruption of the US-appointed Iraqi Governing Council.

After the 7/7 London bombings, Tony Blair promised the British people that he would "bring those responsible to justice." In Iraq, the British government does exactly the opposite. Innocent victims' families are denied the right to bring aggressors to justice, no matter how clearly they can be identified. The law of occupation states that "All foreign soldiers, diplomats or contractors implicated in the killing of Iraqi civilians are immune from arrest or trial in Iraq."

Militias have replaced the disbanded Iraqi army, applying their own rule of law. These include the Iran-based Badr Brigade, al-Chalabi's CIA-trained group, and thousands of foreign mercenaries who entered Iraq after its occupation. Other units operate under a semblance of "legality": the "Wolf Brigade," attached to the ministry of the interior, is infamous for its terror raids on neighborhoods and mosques, and the random imprisonment and torture of civilians.

The British government continues to turn a blind eye to the violations of human rights and murders committed in the name of the "war on terror." While speaking in praise of "democracy," British officials – including the human rights envoy to Iraq – choose to ignore the Vienna Declaration on Human Rights, which proclaims that "Democracy and respect for human rights and fundamental freedoms are inter-dependent and mutually reinforcing."

In a country on the verge of civil war, a new consti-tution has been drawn up. Rather than reflecting the priorities of the Iraqi people, it has been created in order to comply with an imposed timetable aimed at legitimizing the occupation. Under Saddam Hussein, we had a constitution generally described as "pro-gressive and secular." It did not stop him from riding roughshod over human rights. However, the same is true now. The militias of the parties heading the interim government are involved in daily human-rights violations, in particular of women's rights, with the blessing of the occupation.

Most Iraqi women try to cope as best they can with the predicament of dealing with the occupation and the rise of reactionary practices affecting their rights and way of life. For a long time Iraqi women were the most liberated in the Middle East; now, the

US-led occupation has largely confined them to their homes.

A quota system imposed by the US administration controls women's participation in the government, the national assembly and the committee appointed to write the constitution. Iraqi women's historical struggle against colonial domination, and for national unity, social justice and legal equality, has consequently been reduced to bickering among a handful of "women leaders" over nominal political posts.

The silence of female National Assembly members, and interim-government and US-financed women's NGOs, is deafening. In Iraq, discussion of "women's rights" is a charade. Documents released in March 2005 by the American Civil Liberties Union highlight more than a dozen cases of rape and abuse of female detainees. These documents reveal that no action was taken against any soldier or civilian official – and that US troops have destroyed evidence of these abuses, in order to avoid a repetition of the Abu Ghraib scandal. It is no wonder that US-funded NGOs, which preach western-style women's rights and democracy, are regarded as vehicles for foreign manipulation and are widely despised and boycotted.

The architects of the occupation have changed their story after the evident collapse of their Iraqi project. Now, it is Iraqis themselves who are responsible for the mayhem, because they are beyond the reach of democracy. They are "militants" and "insurgents," bent on terrorizing their own people and destroying hopes of reconstruction. Why can't they simply get involved in the peaceful democratic political process?

But the Iraqi people did participate, and continue to do so. Apart from armed resistance – a natural right of nations, according to the 1978 UN general assembly resolution, which reaffirmed "the legitimacy of the struggle of peoples for independence . . . from . . . foreign occupation by all available means, particularly armed struggle" – many other forms of resistance are taking place.

The Iraqi National Foundation Congress (INFC), an umbrella organization of academics, cross-sectarian clerics and veteran political leaders, is leading the political resistance. There is also civil and community resistance involving mosques, women's organizations such as Women's Will, human-rights groups and unions (the Southern Oil Company Union), which are linking up with international anti-war groups and anti-globalization movements.

Over the last three years there have been protests, appeals, initiatives to set up a reasonable program for elections, the opening of human rights centers, lectures at universities, even poetry-writing. This outpouring of activism continues through a broad variety of political parties, groups and individuals who oppose the foreign occupation.

And they have been ignored. Newspapers have been closed; editors arrested. Demonstrators have been shot at, arrested, abused and tortured. In January 2006, the journalist Abdul Hadi al-Zaidi publicly accused government militias of targeting intellectuals. Al-Zaidi is one of a group of Iraqi journalists who, in the aftermath of the Na'as assassination, went on strike. This group is demanding an immediate investigation into the "systematic assassination campaign" targeting intellectuals, seeing it as a concerted attempt to silence and intimidate voices of opposition to the occupation.

But peaceful protest is futile in the face of US torture, killing and collective punishment of civilians; consequently, support for the Iraqi armed resistance is growing amongst the people. The occupiers' claims that these militias are largely "Saddam loyalists" or foreign fighters have been shown to be false. Most fighters in Iraq are Iraqis who are outraged to see their country's resources ransacked while they live in poverty, drink water mixed with sewage and have no say in the political process. The resistance is so persistent and entrenched that the occupying forces' observation of Falluja that "We could take the city, but we would have to destroy it," now applies to many towns and cities throughout Iraq. It has become obvious that the occupation forces, with their elite marine troops, sophisticated weaponry and $6-billion-a-month budget, cannot hold Iraq long – and cannot hope that their pitiful stooges will be able to do so in their place. The only honorable and realistic way out is genuine dialogue with the Iraqi resistance over a total withdrawal of foreign troops, and adequate compensation to rebuild the country.

Most Iraqis believe that they have a right to more than a semblance of independence. The lesson history taught us in Vietnam, that stubborn national resistance can wear down the most powerful armies, is now being learned in Iraq.

MICHEL FABER

Dreams in the Dumpster,
Language Down the Drain

WE WRITERS operate on the assumption that
language matters. And then we're endlessly
slapped in the face with evidence that it doesn't.
Actions speak louder. And violent actions speak loud-
est of all.

Remember when the new millennium dawned?
Language seemed to matter to a great many people
then, especially those pedants who conducted long
disputes in the letters pages of newspapers about
whether the millennium started in 2000 or 2001. The
less anally retentive were more effusive about what the
new century would mean. Journalists, philosophers,
churchmen and politicians expressed their dismay
at the savagery of the twentieth century and predicted that in the future we would be too wise, too
well-informed, too damn war-weary to commit such
atrocities again. With the fall of the Berlin Wall and
the end of the Soviet Union there was a lot of talk of

the supposed inevitability of a more adaptive, caring globalization; several long-running civil wars in Africa had finally ended; a number of the twentieth century's more infamous dictators were doddery, disgraced or both; the Irish peace process seemed viable at last; and there were nuclear accords between the USA and Russia.

Within a few short years, those same pundits were talking about a very different kind of "new world order," which could only be forged by bombing, shooting, incarcerating and terrorizing human beings. Newspapers were spouting Edwardian bluster about cheering on our brave fighting boys. Armchair strategists were predicting that the twenty-first century would be characterized by "us" attacking a succession of "unstable countries" in order to render them harmless. Oil and construction firms squabbled over contracts in post-war Iraq, confident that an unprovoked invasion of an Arab state could be filed away like a bit of paperwork. The British Ministry of Defence trumpeted that the Iraq adventure would be the world's first "clean" war and that there might well be "zero" civilian fatalities. The Iraqis would thank us with joyful hearts for coming to their rescue.

Then the war began, and did what wars do. Who would've thought that the Iraqis would be so resistant to being invaded? Who would've thought that a missile could possibly hit the wrong target? Who would've

thought that a crowded city could have innocent civilians recklessly dwelling in it? Who would've thought
that the enemy leader would hide in a safe place while
his people suffered? Who would've thought that a
country full of bereaved, displaced, harassed and
impoverished citizens would bear a grudge against a
foreign occupying army?

Where did the smart new millennium go?

On the eve of Britain's following the USA into
war, I wrote a letter to Tony Blair, the man who
decides whether to spend my tax money on hospitals
or bombs. Anyone can write a letter to their head of
state. A little girl famously wrote to Abraham Lincoln
and advised him to grow a beard. I didn't advise Tony
Blair to grow a beard, because the prospect of seeing
that manic, insincere grin beaming from inside a dark
mass of hair is most unappealing. Instead, I advised
him thus:

Dear Mr Blair,

You know as well as I do that Saddam Hussein is
extremely unlikely to be hit or even particularly incon-
venienced by the proposed airstrikes. There are 22
million other, more vulnerable inhabitants of Iraq and
they are the ones who will suffer as the war destroys
their homes and their lives. A majority of Iraqis are
children under 14. Those who are not killed will harbor
a wholly understandable grudge against those who
attacked them, which will create generations of terrorists in the future.

If you are concerned about how history will view you as a prime minister, you will earn yourself ignominy if you continue to support the USA's war plans. You will forever be known as the British prime minister who dragged an unwilling nation into war for an ill-defined purpose at the calling of an unusually corrupt and obtuse American president. You are a clever man and I'm sure that underneath the spin you are perfectly aware of the non sequiturs and shaky logic that have led us from the terrorism of September 11 to this war. History has a way of shining a coldly rational light on the events of the past. History books will identify your rhetoric and that of Bush as foolishly belligerent and deceitful, before going on to catalogue the terrible damage done to the world by the war you unleashed.

I appeal to your pride as a politician – please try to salvage your long-term reputation and show yourself to be a statesman. The end will not justify the means. The end will make you a figure of opprobrium.

Yours sincerely,

Michel Faber

See how effective language can be? I'm sure this letter can still be found in Downing Street, or perhaps slightly behind Downing Street, stuck to the clammy interior of a dumpster.

Millions of words have been spent analysing why the governments of Britain and the USA found it convenient or compelling to wage war on Iraq (and, before that, Afghanistan). How many of those words have had any bearing on the willingness or otherwise of young men to join the army and fight, or on the willingness of the general public to tolerate their governments' actions? Very few. In the case of Britain, a one-sentence headline like "Bombs could hit in 45 minutes" just about covers it. In the USA, words weren't even required: all that was needed was endlessly rerun TV footage of two towers being destroyed by aeroplanes. Something bad and scary had happened, caused by ruthless enemies. The USA had to strike back. The striking was the crucial thing, not the words of rationale.

I had the misfortune recently to catch, on someone else's TV, a few minutes of President Bush giving a press conference. A brave journalist dared to ask about the erosion of civil rights by the new "anti-terror" laws. Bush replied, "You don't understand. There are bad people out there, and they want to hurt us." Now, this has always been the implicit message behind the rhetoric of governments when they want to mobilize their country to war. But the message is usually dressed up in statistics, feigned analysis, speechifying – a blizzard of prose. Bush just comes out with it, in all its infant simplicity. Is this the first time we've had a seven-year-old boy as President of the Free World? Or, as my friend Brian Eno suggests, is it more a case of a president assuming a seven-year-old boy's intelligence on the part of his electorate? I don't know how cunning George Bush really is, but one thing is for sure:

language is unimportant to him. He leaves that to the speechwriters, and concentrates on non-verbal symbols, like posing on aircraft carriers. Even the footage of him smugly playing golf while disaster engulfs the world – which so enraged his detractors – gives out a powerful message to those who have no patience with words and moral complexities and clever talk. The message is: we're gonna keep on doin' what we're doin', and everything will be OK.

Language gurgles down the drain; the scars from actions remain. In February 2003, John Brady Kiesling, a member of Bush's Foreign Service Corps and Political Counsellor to the American embassy in Greece, handed in his resignation to US Secretary of State Colin Powell. Kiesling had been a diplomat for twenty years, serving four Presidents. With deep sadness he spoke of the way America was squandering its international legitimacy, dismantling its international relationships, spreading disproportionate terror and confusion in the public mind. His letter of protest was a masterpiece of dignity, eloquent reasoning, astute analysis and, most of all, humanity. I urge you all to seek it out and read it. God knows why, because nobody remembers who the hell John Brady Kiesling was, if they ever took note in the first place. His letter of resignation, wonderful and humbling though it is, is mere words. Dead children are actions. Burning buildings are actions. Missiles are actions.

Checkpoints and torture cells and rioting fanatics are actions.

A few years ago, I wrote a novella called *Bombshell*, a distillation of all my rage and disappointment over Britain's behaviour in following the USA into war. My publisher refused to publish it, not because he disagreed with its politics, but because he didn't think it was good enough. I sympathize with those aesthetics. As it happens, I disagreed with my publisher about the quality of *Bombshell*, but I didn't have what it took to hawk the novella to a rival publisher. I still wonder sometimes whether I did the right thing. Might my carefully aimed literary weapon have had an impact on the British public? Then I remind myself: words don't stop wars. Words are there to bring us back to an illusion of sanity after wars have done their worst.

I am both proud and ashamed to be in the business of articulating that illusion.

All royalties from the sales of *Not One More Death*
will go to the Stop the War Coalition